Silent Chords

Between the Lines of Love

Dr. Anisha N.

BookLeaf Publishing

India | USA | UK

Made with ❤ on the BookLeaf Publishing Platform
www.bookleafpub.in
www.bookleafpub.com

Dedication

Dedicated to Vishnu Peethambaran

Preface

This anthology is my debut attempt at capturing the myriad hues of love through poetry. Each of the 21 poems in this collection delves into a different phase of love, from its tender beginnings to its enduring strength, from moments of joy to the bittersweet pangs of longing. As a novice, this endeavor has been both challenging and rewarding. These verses stem from personal reflections and emotions, weaving a narrative that I hope will resonate with every reader who has ever loved or been loved.

I invite you to step into this world of love—its beauty, its struggles, and its pain. Whether you find echoes of your own experiences or discover new perspectives, I hope these poems touch your heart and kindle your own reflections on love.

Warm regards,

Dr Anisha N.

Acknowledgements

I extend my heartfelt gratitude to my husband for his unwavering support and encouragement throughout this journey. I am also deeply thankful to my colleagues, whose guidance have nurtured my novice attempts at poetry. This being my debut anthology, their belief in my work has been a source of inspiration while crafting these 21 poems of love.

1. Wood Rose

The wood rose stands aloof
apart from the vibrant
throngs of colorful roses.

The butterfly flits, gazing
at each bloom,
smiling foolishly, making
every rose believe
it holds his heart.

Yet the wood rose,
devoid of fragrance,
lacking sweet nectar to offer,
painted within herself
a vivid portrait of him-
her butterfly.

She bore witness to his changes,
a moth no more,
emerging from the cocoon

to steal her heart.

Alas! the butterfly sought only hues
unwilling to embrace
the wood rose's steadfast loyalty.

Untouched by filth or greed,
wood rose shed her petals,
finally cradled by the soothing
hands of the gale,
who held her close,
pressed gently against his heart.

2. Morning Wisdom

When morning unfolds its petals,
I find joy in the sunlight,
eager to witness blooms heavy
with the aches and thorns of love.

Nature summons a journey-
an infinite palette of wonders,
inviting the soul to plunge deep
into the wisdom of seas and oceans.

Boundless, unyielding,
caressing the heart of its lover,
untouched by contempt or weariness,
the breeze whispers softly,
brushing against the flower's soul,
holding the stems in tender embrace.

Rain pours unceasingly,
much like my love- endless,
for the one I hold dear.

3. Mythopoeia

I soared among the towering peaks,
unburdened, weightless,
drifting through veils of cloud.

Far beyond the thorns and shadows
of fractured love and painted facades,
I brushed against feathers pure as dawn,
drank the whispers of rain,
listened to the thunder's solemn hymn.

No pain could pierce my stillness-
for my ears are hushed,
my voice a silent sentinel.

Yet, within the stillness, music stirs-
melodies of a forgotten past,
chords once faded now resound,
brimming with plundered joy.

I am nature's silent beauty,

the guardian of its timeless wisdom,
an endless symphony,
harmonizing the wild and the serene.

4. Coffee Date

Playing with the latte art heart,
I lost myself in countless images,
never once meeting his gaze.

Moody with the thoughts of
the one who shattered
my soul into pieces,
hushed by emotions, I
brood over dreams long lost.

He, so considerate
despite his weariness,
his eyes heavy from a long journey,
strain to hear my broken chords.
"Talk to me, Padma, I am
the one always speaking",
he pleads-

"Aadhi", I said softly,
I have given away my voice."

Steadying me, he clasps my hand,
"Your eyes", he murmurs,
"Hold a world where I never let you
drown in the ocean of tears."

The cycle of promises echoes
through me, weaving
a web of mockery.

I look around seeking
the butterfly I've always
adored, alas! it remains
nowhere to be found.

5. Silence

My soft whimpering
soothes your ears, my tears
draw you to ecstasy.

Over the years, you battered
my heart with unromantic fervour,
blurring the line between pain and joy.

I crawled in your shadow,
haunted by the silence you
wielded,
enchanted by the storm
in your gaze.

The beauty of the world
became ashes to me,
dimmed by the obsession
you left in your wake.
Yet, you barely saw me.

Loyalty, a fleeting mirage,
mocked me with its radiant smile
for I had lavished it upon
A sea of indifference,
upon the soul, I once
called my beloved!

6. Distance

Perhaps the moon
once loved the sun,
believing in the illusion
of their eternal union-
day and night, only to be
abandoned in the dark.

The moon , blind to
the gentle gaze of little stars,
oblivious to the chasm
between moon and sun,
with devotion through the ages,
unaware of time slipping away.

Swelling with pride, transforming
into fullness and emptiness,
the moon dons its foolish charades
to please his beloved.
How more ages will this go on?

7. Stream

Out in the woods
I lay on the meadows
whispering to the shadows
around me; I feel engrossed
in the wilderness
forgetting the past
filled with the chords
of melancholy.

Rain of happiness
covered me, a peaceful
retreat nowhere to be found.

Butterflies fluttered around
seeking the nectar,
pricked me; in the wild
ecstasy of pain and pleasure,
amidst the musings of rain-

whispered to me
to fill the swollen eyes with
the silver lining of sky;
to embrace the dawn,
to befriend the moon, and
to listen to the farewell
symphony of cricket.

The once clouded
eyes could now vividly portray
the beauty of the silent stream.

8. Song of Pain

You scorched away
my long stricken cancer with
the flames of your neglect...
In dreams, bearing the fatherhood of my innocence,
you carried the songs of crafted visions
to the infinite slumber.
If I had held you only in my hands,
perhaps, dear heart,
you wouldn't have shattered so.
The eyes that slipped away,
and the days that are now lost to time
might be alien to you now.
When kisses lost in oblivion
shrink into tears,
disgust, and grievances in you,
I awaken to the realization:
love has aged.
And so have I,

who was born before you.
Now, to see me,
you need glasses.
To remember me,
you need my messages.
And to caress me,
your hands now require strength.
In love, you sought selfishness,
forgetting the world where
you were me,
and I was you.
When silence estranges sleep,
words perform the music of deception.

9. Waiting

In the sheath of a tiny flower lies hidden
a nectar sweet, like honey divine,
like the stars veiled behind dark clouds,
your face I have hidden in my eyes.

Your gentle voice my heart embraced,
transforming into the rhythm of my soul.
Day and night have drifted apart,
you remain but as dreams alone.

Words have deserted me today,
And my thoughts, dear one,
are solely of you.
Today, I am no more!
Within me, I seek your spirit,
and every moment, you throb within me.
Unknowingly, I wait for you still.

10. Chamber of secrets

While arranging my files with care,
I opened a hidden cover of chocolates,
a treasure concealed from the world.
Gently patting its soft surface,
I inhaled its scent—
and found you lingering there.

Ah... each day, my fingers reached for it,
and now it carries only my fragrance.
Tears welled and spilled—
Why did I touch it so often?
Why did I let your enchanting scent fade?

I felt the slow erosion of you,
Like whispers slipping through time.
The hidden treasure in almirah,
where no one could touch,

no one could see—
for I kept you deep within.
Deep in the chambers of
my weeping heart,
once proud of your love,
now torn apart,
draped in oblivion.

11. Chasing Shadows

I fell in love
with the letters
of your sweet little hands

Collecting all the broken
pages of your book,
I reread the errors
of my eyes, so clouded
and ignorant,
fumbled at the meanings
of the infinte world
created by your words.

The dark new world
where light fears to enter,
I drew the many faces of you.

12. Laughing Butterfly

When I first opened my eyes,
I saw a butterfly with wings
painted in vibrant colors,
holding me close to its heart.

The petals and leaves, unaware,
watched the butterfly with love.
The flower, full of hope,
waited as the butterfly
gifted its young to her embrace.

As the petals began to wither and fall,
the flower sat waiting,
longing for the butterfly to return.

The flower, devoted to one alone,
cursed her own love as foolishness.
Even when surrounded by other blossoms,
she felt abandoned and solitary.
Yet, forgetting the pain of her solitude,

she stayed awake,
yearning for her beloved forever.

In the unquenchable memories of you,
though I may fade,
will I still remain as a distorted shadow?

13. The Lost Symphony

You once whispered,
"Kannaa, I love thee so much..."
Echoed in my ears and
etched in the heart,
a precious world mirrored.
Through the ache of unending letters,
thy hand grew weary,
while my tear-laden eyes
found sanctuary in your songs.
But alas, as you did slowly fade,
my laughter too fell silent.
The portraits you painted in my soul
now wane, their colors dimmed to shadows.
Lonely nights unfurl once more,
carrying the weight
of a lover's uncertain heart,
earning for the melody of thy voice.

The songs that once lulled me to rest
now cradle another's dreams.

14. Illusion

Some people are like night!
Unseen by others...
offering dreams,
weaving rainbows with words,
they take us along.

Days adorn them
with new forms and meanings.
In the falsehood that night and day are one,
they gift us a mask of naivety.
Unaware of the truth—
we are left alone at dawn.

Even tears are painted with rainbows,
as we wait for the night.

When life is shrouded in frost,
unable to discern night from day;

in a heart writhing with pain,
unknowingly try to sever blind love.
Chasing futile dreams,
embarking on a journey
into the infinite world
to bring them to life.

15. You

Nothing as vast as you,
nor as profound—
fill my memory.

Your eyes unfathomable,
a puzzle unsolved.
I see a saint and lover
distant and near.
In the garden of
my dreams, I nourish
you with tears and
breath of my soul.

16. Silent Hymns

The tree and the bird
souls so different,
with distances infinite.

When your fragile wings
tire in flight,
I'll soothe and cradle you
with my tender leaves;
and offer you shade,
a shelter with my branches.

Your silent sorrows,
your trembling heart—
without the need for words,
I've woven them deeply
into the veins of my soul.

With no language to speak,

only a heartbeat to guide,
I've held my love for you
like a treasure untouched.

Through endless years,
I've shaped myself
in the image of you.
As you soar across the vastness,
you are all I think of.

I'll wait in eternity
to touch those radiant feathers,
to hear that breath once more,
to gather the infinite thoughts
you've left behind,
like a prayer whispered
through lifetimes.

17. Obsession

The love that walked beside
me like a shadow;
sank deep into my heart,
hiding its silent sobs
where no one could hear.

A glance, a smile—
in it's fleeting grace,
I found boundless joy.

The yearnings of my heart
gleamed like distant stars,
that light up only the quiet of night.

In solitude and in stillness,
I wove your voice into
the rhythm of my heart,
savoring alone

that unspoken, silent love.

And now, without my knowing,
it has flowed from my hands to yours.

By the will of fate,
like stars that shimmer
in endless eternity,
I stand sleepless,
forever waiting for
the radiant light.

18. Black Sheep

Alone in the crowd
lost amidst desert roses,
drifting aimlessly,
a fleeting shadow in a vast
white cloud,scuttling
towards a distant mirage.

I watch as rain descends,
softly plundering the parched soil,
it's fragrance unfurling—
a tender balm to earth's wounds.

Like a child chasing butterflies,
petals weave themselves
into a kaleidoscopic vision;
dancing with the gentle breeze.

And the soul, once scarred
by the thorns of long-lost love,

blooms anew.
Each wound a brushstroke
in the portrait of resilience.

19. Hollow Eyes

I loved reading the messages
hidden in your eyes,
floating through the colors
of your little, vivid worlds.

At first, they gleamed,
radiant and alive,
But slowly, they faded away.

Once, I could decipher them
with ease, without pain.
Now, with tearful eyes,
I see only emptiness.

What was once a vibrant story
is now a hollow frame—
a reflection of your
vanishing soul.

20. Agony

When the tender touch
of a tiny breeze
caressed the fading
flower's crown...
with a soft sigh,
it hid its tears.
In the fleeting breeze
that drifted away
lingered the silent
sob and fragrance of
the little flower...

The bee, savoring its nectar,
knew not of the life
that had merged into its breath.

21. Cactus

Though looks beautiful,
with its long-awaited bloom;
once in a while,
eyes meet the full eclipse,
longing for an embrace,
adorned with thorns.

Days yearn for roses—
yellows and reds—
amid green leaves,
wide and narrow.

Dreams dance
in the wilderness,
drenched and smothered
by the pain of love.

9 789369 546107